Follow Your Dream

Follow your Dream

Edited by Tina Hacker

Illustrations by David Welty

HALLMARK EDITIONS

The publisher wishes to thank those who have given their kind permission to reprint material included in this book. Every effort has been made to give proper acknowledgments. Any omissions or errors are deeply regretted, and the publisher, upon notification, will be pleased to make necessary corrections in subsequent editions.

ACKNOWLEDGMENTS: "How to Find Adventure" from *The Stars at Noon* by Jacqueline Cochran. Copyright © 1954 by Jacqueline Cochran. Reprinted by permission of the author. "Knowledge" from *The Open Door* by Helen Keller. Copyright © 1957 by Helen Keller. Reprinted by permission of the publisher, Doubleday & Company, Inc. "Keep on Growing" from *Loretta Lynn: Coal Miner's Daughter* by Loretta Lynn with George Vecsey. © 1976 by Loretta Lynn. Reprinted with permission of Bernard Geis Associates, Inc. "The Fun Shouldn't Stop" excerpted from the article "Telly Savalas — Is He Really Kojak?" an interview by Katharine Balfour from the August, 1976, issue of *Family Circle*. Copyright © 1976, The Family Circle, Inc., and reprinted with their permission. "The Best Way" by Clarence "Biggie" Munn excerpted from *Guideposts Magazine*. Copyright 1953 by Guideposts Associates, Inc., Carmel, N.Y. 10512. Used with permission. "Something of Our Own" by Lola Redford and "Always Better" by Eve Queler from *Women Today* by Greta Walker. © 1975 by Greta Walker. Reprinted by permission of the publisher, Hawthorn Books, Inc. "The Skyline Is a Promise" and "Dream your dreams..." from *The Skyline Is a Promise* by Guilford Dudley, Jr. © 1965 by Guilford Dudley, Jr. Reprinted with permission of the author. "Believing in Yourself" by Liberace. Reprinted by permission of the author. "The Journey to Tomorrow" from *Harvest of Yesterdays* by Gladys Taber. Copyright © 1976 by Gladys Taber. Reprinted by permission of J. B. Lippincott Company. "A Measure of Success" and "The river flows..." reprinted with permission of Macmillan Publishing Co., Inc. from *Successful Living Day by Day* by Nelson Boswell. Copyright © 1972 by Nelson Boswell. "Only Beginnings" reprinted by permission of William Morrow & Co., Inc. from *Dear America* by Karl Hess. Copyright © 1975 by Karl Hess. "Nothing Boring in Life" and "I have never..." by Nadia Boulanger reprinted from *Wisdom for Our Time*, edited by James Nelson, by permission of W. W. Norton & Company, Inc. Copyright © 1961 by National Broadcasting Company, Inc. "Courage" and "An Awareness of Truth" reprinted from *The Courage to Create* by Rollo May, by permission of W. W. Norton & Company, Inc. and William Collins Sons & Co., Ltd. Copyright © 1975 by Rollo May. "The Greatest Championship" by Jesse Owens reprinted by permission of the author. "A Better Life" by Bill Talcott and "Determination" by Dave Bender from *Working: People Talk About What They Do All Day and How They Feel About What They Do*, by Studs Terkel. Copyright © 1972, 1974 by Studs Terkel. Reprinted by permission of Pantheon Books, a Division of Random House, Inc. and Wildwood House, Ltd. "Anything Is Possible" by S. J. Diamond condensed from the November 22, 1976, issue of *People Weekly* Magazine by special permission. © 1976, Time Inc. All rights reserved. "Stuff You Can't Buy" by Elizabeth Ashley from *The Success Trip* by Ross Firestone. © 1976 by Ross Firestone. Reprinted by permission of Playboy Press and Ross Firestone. "Anchors or Steppingstones" from the book *How to Enjoy Work and Get More Fun Out of Life* by O. A. Battista, Sc.D. © 1957 by O. A. Battista. Reprinted by permission of the publisher, Prentice-Hall, Inc., Englewood Cliffs, New Jersey. "A Step Forward" from the book *My America, Your America* by Lawrence Welk with Bernice McGeehan. © 1976 by Lawrence Welk. Reprinted by permission of the publisher, Prentice-Hall, Inc., Englewood Cliffs, New Jersey. "Looking Ahead" from the book *Road to a Richer Life* by Walter B. Pitkin. © 1949 by Prentice-Hall, Inc. Reprinted by permission of the publisher, Prentice-Hall, Inc., Englewood Cliffs, New Jersey. "Everything Is Easy" reprinted by permission of G. P. Putnam's Sons and Brandt & Brandt from *Writing Without Rules* by Robert E. Lee. Originally published in *Daily Variety*. Copyright © 1976 by Robert E. Lee. Selection from "The Neglected Art of Being Different" in *A Touch of Wonder* by Arthur Gordon, published by Fleming H. Revell Company. Originally appeared in *Reader's Digest*. Copyright © 1963 by Readers Digest Association. "A Special Privilege" by Rudyard Kipling from "Interview With an Immortal" in *A Touch of Wonder* by Arthur Gordon, published by Fleming H. Revell Company. Originally appeared in *Reader's Digest*. Copyright © 1959 by Readers Digest Association. "Always a New Purpose" from *Survival Plus* by Reuel L. Howe. Copyright © 1971 by Reuel L. Howe. Reprinted by permission of the publisher, The Seabury Press. "Everybody Is a Star" by Kevin Hooks as told to Edwin Miller. Reprinted from *SEVENTEEN®* Magazine. Copyright © 1976 by Triangle Communications Inc. All rights reserved. Reprinted by permission. "Say Yes to Yourself" quoting Cindy Williams from an article by Edwin Miller. Reprinted from *SEVENTEEN®* Magazine. Copyright © 1976 by Triangle Communications Inc. All rights reserved. Reprinted by permission. "Fighting Back" from the book *Fighting Back*. Copyright © 1975 by Rocky Bleier and Terry O'Neil. Reprinted with permission of Stein and Day Publishers. "The Need to Create" from *Heroes* by Joe McGinniss. Copyright © 1976 by JoeMac, Inc. Reprinted by permission of The Viking Press and Sterling Lord Agency, Inc.

© 1978, Hallmark Cards, Inc., Kansas City, Missouri.
Printed in the United States of America. Standard Book Number: 87529-539-8.

Follow Your Dream

THE SUREST GUIDES

Ideals are like stars: you will not succeed in touching them with your hands, but like the seafaring man on the desert of waters, you choose them as your guides, and following them, you reach your destiny.

AUTHOR UNKNOWN

A Better Life

All human recorded history is about five thousand years old. How many people in all that time have made an overwhelming difference? Twenty? Thirty? Most of us spend our lives trying to achieve some things. But we're not going to make an overwhelming difference. We do the best we can. That's enough.

The problem with history is that it's written by college professors about great men. That's not what history is. History's a...lot of little people getting together and deciding they want a better life for themselves and their kids.

Bill Talcott

How to Find Adventure

Jacqueline Cochran's life has certainly been an exciting one! Besides being a prosperous businesswoman, she was the first woman to fly a jet faster than the speed of sound and the first woman to make a blind landing. Her formula for success?? Ambition and honesty blended with faith.

I have found that it is as easy to reach for the moon as it is to reach for the top of the fence that hems you in — if one mixes ambition and imagination. Of course, the mixture must contain a base of honesty, and the whole must be blended with faith....

I became the first woman to pass the sonic barrier and to exceed the speed of sound. That meant a climb to an altitude of nearly 50,000 feet. Up there, even by day, the sky is dark blue, and the stars can be seen. Earthbound friends are left behind....

Flying through the sound barrier is like flying inside an explosion. In the dive the plane creates a shock wave, and when it pulls out of the dive the shock wave speeds straight down toward earth, and strikes the earth with two whip-crack explosions. In my first dive these explosions were heard on the flight line, but were not recorded in the observation tower. I was heartsick. That same day, however, I went back up again and repeated the dive so they could be recorded properly. Two weeks later I did it again.

I have found adventure in flying, in world travel, in business and even close at hand. There can be adventure in such a simple pastime as my helping the wild quail on our ranch lose their fear and come trustfully close to me.

Adventure is a state of mind — and spirit. It comes through faith — for with complete faith there is no fear of what faces one in life or death.

there's always more beauty
to be discovered....

Always Better

Eve Queler, pianist and conductor, shares her views about the value of music. But, indeed, this philosophy can be applied to any endeavor a person believes in.

There's always something new to be found in the music. There's always more beauty to be discovered. There's no time when you can say, "Well, this is it." You can't re-create a performance. The next one will be different. That one is over, but the next one will always be better. It must be.

Life's Little Tests

We don't need the courage to face life's big tests. What we need is courage to meet life's little tests. What we need is the courage to follow a regular routine, the courage to stick to our plans, the courage to keep the petty irritations of the day from blocking our efforts, the courage to keep on going hour after hour. We need to remember that it isn't the big trees that trip us up as we walk through the forest, but the vines on the ground, the exposed roots, the low underbrush.

Clay Hamlin

The Neglected Art of Being Different

One of the most vivid and painful recollections of my life concerns... a hat.

When I was eleven, my parents sent me to a summer camp run along semimilitary lines. Part of each camper's uniform was supposed to be a boy-scout hat, low-crowned, wide-brimmed, to be worn every afternoon without fail when we lined up for formal inspection.

But my parents did not provide me with a scout hat. Through some catastrophic oversight, they sent me off with one of those army campaign hats, vintage of 1917. It was wide-brimmed, all right: when I put it on, I was practically in total darkness....Whenever I wore this hat, instead of being an inconspicuous and somewhat homesick small boy, I became a freak.

Or so I thought. Looking back now, across the years, I can smile at the memory of my wan little face peering out forlornly from under that monstrosity of a hat. But it was no joke at the time. I was miserable — utterly, abjectly miserable. Why? Because I was *different,* different from the others, different from the crowd....

The fear of being different, like most fears, tends to diminish when you drag it into the light and take a good look at it. At the bottom of such fear lies an intense preoccupation with self. That comical hat, back in my childhood, might have caused some momentary merriment or temporary teasing. But the whole thing was too trivial to have lasted long. I was the one who kept it alive by agonizing about it....

It takes courage to be different, but there is also an art to it, the art of not antagonizing people unnecessarily by your differentness. People don't object to differentness nearly so much as they object to the attitude of superiority that so often goes with it....

The rule of thumb is very simple: Be as different as you like, but try to be tolerant of the people who differ from you. If we all granted to one another the right simply to be ourselves, we would be different enough. When he was eight years old, someone asked Henry Thoreau what he was going to be when he grew up. "Why," said the boy, "I will be I!" He was, too.

Arthur Gordon

Dream your dreams, then blueprint your dreams, and finally contract with yourself to construct them stone by stone. But while you are dreaming, DREAM BIG!

GUILFORD DUDLEY, JR.

Everything Is Easy

Playwright and author Robert E. Lee offers some words of wisdom for the aspiring writer. But his advice is really universal and can be applied to almost any career, any goal. Here Mr. Lee tells why he thinks "everything is easy."

When the Old Rabbi of Minsk was dying, thousands of people lined up outside his house to learn what would be the last words of this great and wise man. The doctor leaned over the bed and asked: "Rabbi, is there one last word of wisdom that you want to give the people of Minsk?"

The old man nodded, and very weakly he said: *"Life is an empty rain barrel!"*

Rapidly the word went down the line to the people outside. "The Rabbi says: 'Life is an empty rain barrel...' etc." A little man at the end of the line heard this and he said: "Wait a minute, what does he mean, life is an empty rain barrel?" So the word started to go back along the line: "What does he mean, life is an empty rain barrel?" Finally, the doctor leaned over the bed again, and said:

"Rabbi, we're sorry to bother you while you're dying... but what do you mean: 'Life is an empty rain barrel'?"

Long pause. Then the Rabbi said: "So, life is *not* an empty rain barrel."

There are two morals to this story.

In most wisdom, the *reverse* is also true.

You have been taught that writing is hard. I tell you that writing is so hard that you will probably never write anything unless you think of it as easy!

Secondly, I think the old Rabbi was right the first time.

I don't mean to drench you with hydraulic metaphors. But, for a writer, life *is* an empty rain barrel.

Because you can't catch any rain in a FULL rain barrel!!!

It is a permeating principle of Hindu Theology: that a man must *empty* himself before he can *fill* himself.

Writing...art...the entire creative process is something which comes from somewhere outside the person of the artist. You are a vessel — as Paul says, an earthen vessel — a fragile vehicle — through which a precious essence is poured.

And if you resist — tense up — worry — doubt — fear — encrust your script with apprehension over the difficulty of what you're trying to do —

You constrict the flow, and nothing happens...!

You can't water the roses if you're standing on the hose!

If you turn military, become a slave of regulations and rules, bark orders at yourself — I doubt if you'll win any battles.

Open up...relax...have faith in your strength and your source...let it come, let it flow through you.

Empty yourself, so you can be inspired anew!

Who knows?

You may discover that the *lie* I've been telling you is really true...THAT EVERYTHING IS EASY!!!

Something of Our Own

Lola Redford, cofounder of CAN — Consumer Action Now — talks about the importance of relying on one's own self and having one's own identity. For her, as for most people, this is a feat that is never simple.

Although I don't get paid for working with CAN — whatever we make on lectures goes back into the organization — I do like the idea of earning my own money. When I think of the book we're doing, I think how nice it would be if we made money on it and each of the women could have some money of her own. There's a sense of pride in earning your own way. It's been a long time since I've done that. Although it's not necessary for the upkeep of my household, there's something freeing psychologically about it. You know that if anything happens you can take care of yourself.

Having my own life has made it easier for my husband. He's relieved of the responsibility of having to create an ego for me. He knows that the things I'm doing are making me very happy and I don't have to rely on the things he will bring me.

We should all have something of our own. We should have something of our own because we're all here alone.... You really have to go through the traumas of life by yourself. No one, even when you're married and have children, is going to help you when it gets down to that final crunch. No one can. It's what you're made of that's going to make whatever experience you run into either a positive experience for you or something that takes you down. To be able to rely on oneself in all sorts of circumstances and to put yourself in a position where you can test things out are both very good and positive.

Nothing Boring in Life

Nadia Boulanger, internationally known musician, scholar and teacher, talks about work and her view that all kinds of work can be worthwhile and interesting if we have the right attitude.

There is nothing boring in life except ourselves. The most humble work does not have to be boring. I remember the old woman who cleaned the floor in my place in Gargenville. She died years ago. Every day I think of her with the most profound respect and with the greatest reverence. She was eighty years old. One day she knocked at my door and said, "Mademoiselle, I know you don't like to be disturbed, but the floor, come and see it, it shines in such a way." Now I always think of her. In my mind, Stravinsky and Madame Duval will appear before the Lord for the same reason. Each has done what he does with all his consciousness. When I said to Madame Duval, "You, Madame Duval, when you die, you will appear to the Lord as equal to Mr. Stravinsky, and for the same reasons." She did not know exactly what I meant. She could not understand. But when I said the same thing to Stravinsky, who knew her, he said, "How you flatter me, for when I do something, I have something to gain. I have something. But she, she has only the work to be well done."

KNOWLEDGE

"Knowledge is power." Rather, knowledge is happiness, because to have knowledge — broad, deep knowledge — is to know true ends from false, and lofty things from low. To know the thoughts and deeds that have marked man's progress is to feel the great heartthrobs of humanity through the centuries; and if one does not feel in these pulsations a heavenward striving, one must indeed be deaf to the harmonies of life.

HELEN KELLER

The Greatest Championship

There are four things that I feel are important factors in determining a winning attitude. First of all, in our dreams and as we climb the ladder to those dreams, each rung in that ladder has a very definite meaning. The first rung is your determination to your dream. The next rung is your dedication to your dream. The third rung in that ladder is the self-discipline that you must display and the sacrifice that goes with it. The fourth rung in the ladder is the kind of attitude that you assume in reaching your dream. We all strive for the top rung of the ladder, and that's the thing that is called championship. Championship is the ultimate for all of us, but we must remember that championships are very symbolic.

Now what is important on the road to that championship? To me, we must learn to spell the word RESPECT. We must respect the rights and properties of our fellowman. And then learn to play the game of life, as well as the game of athletics, according to the rules of our society.

If you can take that and put it into practice in the community in which you live, then, to me, you have won the greatest championship that any person can ever win, because these are the things that will never gather dust, and these are the things that will never become tarnished, and these are the things that will live with you as long as you live on the face of God's earth.

Jesse Owens

Anchors or Steppingstones

Mistakes can be anchors that drag you down, or steppingstones to greater levels of achievement. Unless you take the proper *attitude* toward mistakes, however, you are doomed to lose much of the pleasure from your work. No matter how successful you may appear to be on the outside, real and lasting satisfaction comes only from inside of you. The most important point of all to remember about mistakes is this: *No error becomes a mistake until you refuse to correct it.*

O. A. Battista

Keep on Growing

I don't know what it's like for a book writer or a doctor or a teacher as they work to get established in their jobs. But for a singer, you've got to continue to grow or else you're just like last night's cornbread — stale and dry.

Loretta Lynn

Adventure is where you find it,
and you can find it anywhere....

Anything Is Possible

If you ask a child what he wants to do when he grows up, you might get a response anywhere from driving a fire engine to landing on Mars. John Goddard set 127 goals for himself! Unlike most, these goals were not mere childhood musings. Here S. J. Diamond describes some of the many goals Mr. Goddard has already achieved.

Even at 15, John Goddard knew what he wanted to do with his life. One rainy morning in 1940 the ambitious Los Angeles teen-ager wrote down 127 goals on a pad of yellow paper. Some represented the simplest adolescent longings: to high-jump 5 feet, broad-jump 15 feet, do 200 sit-ups and 20 pull-ups, and weigh a trim 175 pounds. Others were a little more demanding. He wanted to explore the Nile, fly in a blimp, light a match with a .22 rifle. He was determined to climb the Matterhorn, ride an ostrich and read the Bible from cover to cover.

So far Goddard, 52, now a professional adventurer-lecturer, has achieved each of these goals and more — 105 in all — while traveling the equivalent of 40 times around the world. In the process he has been chased by a warthog (while photographing Rhodesia's Victoria Falls), bitten by a diamondback rattler (while milking it for venom) and nearly buried alive in an African sandstorm.

To be sure, there have been disappointments. He has not climbed Mount Everest (No. 21), become a ham radio operator (No. 95) or owned a cheetah (No. 94). Nor has he read the entire Encyclopaedia Britannica

(No. 109), although he has managed to plow through sizable portions of each thick volume.

Goddard probably won't become a doctor (No. 37) either, but he hasn't given up. "I might still," he says. "I don't believe in retirement." He now regards appearing in a Tarzan movie (No. 93) as a silly boyhood dream. Getting to the moon (No. 125) seems improbable, and Goddard will realize his final goal — to see the 21st century — only if he lives to be 75. For Goddard, living as long as he has seems a miracle, considering adventures like his kayak-and-canoe voyage down the Congo River 20 years ago. It took six weeks to travel the first 450 miles and 127 rapids. During one watery spill, his partner, Jack Yowall, drowned. "We had made a pact," Goddard recalls, "that if one of us was killed, the other would finish."

Exploring the Nile back in 1950 wasn't much easier. Goddard and two French companions spent 13 months navigating the great river's 4,187 miles....

Goddard continues to work his way through the list. In the next few months he expects to learn to play polo (No. 122) and visit Easter Island (No. 57). "Life should be a series of adventures," Goddard declares in words that have the ring of another, simpler era. "Boredom is responsible for a great deal of our juvenile — and adult — delinquency. People should reach for their potential. Adventure is where you find it, and you can find it anywhere."

The Fun Shouldn't Stop

Here actor Telly Savalas tells how his mother's opinions have shaped his attitudes toward success. Telly is having fun now and doesn't plan to stop even if his success "dies down."

"Get on with it, Telly," she [his mother] says. "Stop taking the bows and listening to the applause. Get off that merry-go-round and get on to something more important." Well, you get caught up in success and I'm having fun with it, living every day to the fullest. But that great lady also gave me the awareness that one day the applause will stop. And you can rest assured that I'm prepared for that as well. And when it all dies down and I'm no longer a sex symbol, if that's what I am, when they've got some new stiff up there, then Telly's going to be having fun in another area.

A Special Privilege

Rudyard Kipling is well known for his wise words of advice to mankind. Here Arthur Gordon relates some of that advice from a conversation he had with Kipling.

The individual has always had to struggle to keep from being overwhelmed by the tribe. To be your own man is a hard business. If you try it, you'll be lonely often, and sometimes frightened. But no price is too high to pay for the privilege of owning yourself.

23

LOOKING AHEAD

Life becomes worth living only
to the man who has learned,
as he surveys the work of the
day just past, to look forward
with enthusiasm to the next
day's tasks. It is the entire
pattern that makes life worth
living. No part of living can
stand for the whole. No
moment of living can take the
place of the long surge and
sweep of living through
the years.

WALTER B. PITKIN

The Best Way

Nature provides so many relaxing pleasures if we but care to take the time to see them.

When the pressures and demands on my time are keeping me away from my wife and children, in my schedule will appear such items as "June 1-8, Canada, Vera and Janey." and "Aug. 6-13, canoe trip, Mike."

Any busy man who doesn't give his family the same billing as a business trip is not giving himself, or his family, a break.

Out of my boyhood struggles and hardships have come a solid sense of values and an appreciation about what is worthwhile in life. I have tried in the best way I know how to communicate my faith and philosophy to my boys, to show them that there are no short cuts, no free rides, and that the hard way is the best way.

Clarence "Biggie" Munn

Determination

"With determination," says Dave Bender, "you can conquer the world." And in a way, he has done just that. He started out with only forty dollars in his pocket and is now the owner of a prosperous factory. Here Mr. Bender talks about his work and how determination still plays a large role in his life.

I like making things. I make the machinery here. I'm not an engineer, but I have an idea and I kind of develop things and — (with an air of wonder) — they *work*. All night long I think about this place. I love my work.

It isn't the money. It's just a way of expressing my feeling....

I'm making a machine now. I do hope to have it ready in the next couple months. The machine has nothing to do with helping humanity in any size, shape, or form. It's a personal satisfaction for me to see this piece of iron doing some work. It's like a robot working. This is the reward itself for me, nothing else. My ego, that's it.

Something last night was buggin' me. I took a sleeping pill to get it out of my mind. I was up half the night just bugging and bugging and bugging. I was down here about six o'clock this morning. I said, "Stop everything. We're making a mistake." I pointed out where the mistake was and they said, "...we never thought of that." Today we're rebuilding the whole thing. This kind of stuff gets me. Not only what was wrong, but how the devil do you fix it? I felt better. This problem, that's over with. There's no problem that can't be solved if you use logic and reason the thing out. I don't care what it is. Good horse sense is what it's known as. With that you can do anything you want— determination, you can conquer the world.

The Skyline Is a Promise

If you have traveled but once, you have certainly felt the inexplicable emotion that hits you when the skyline of a city sweeps suddenly before your eyes. As you reach the crest of the hill or round the steep curve, there it lies filling the horizon.

The striking pinnacles of stone and steel piercing the sky; the dramatic rise and fall of towers to tenements; the mighty steps, some in giant leaps, that climb upward toward dizzying heights, then drop suddenly into deep crevices. Here is Beauty. Here is Power. Here is Majesty. Here also is a Promise — a Promise of rich reward for those who, as John Masefield said, "Go forth to seek"!

Look closely and you can see the skyline paint upon a brilliant blue canvas vivid pictures of those who dwell within the city; of their high success and low failure; the complacency of the many and the ambition of the few; of the wonderful opportunities offered to all but given only to those who try.

Then remember as you cross the horizon and enter the city, the decision is yours. You can remain in the shadows of the towering structures or you can strive to gain the heights. It is really up to you, for certainly "The skyline is a promise, not a bound."

Guilford Dudley, Jr.

*In the mountains of truth,
you never climb in vain.
Either you already reach a
higher point today, or you
exercise your strength in
order to be able to climb
higher tomorrow.*

FRIEDRICH NIETZSCHE

Only Beginnings

You are, we are, human; you have, we have, those unique abilities which can set us free — intuition which can inspire discovery and creativity, and reason which can make it whole and meaningful in the natural world.

There can be, therefore, no end...to the process of being human. There are only beginnings, endless, dawning, wonderful beginnings. And the good work of being people, friends, lovers — and good neighbors.

Karl Hess

An Awareness of Truth

To believe fully and at the same moment to have doubts is not at all a contradiction: it presupposes a greater respect for truth, an awareness that truth always goes beyond anything that can be said or done at any given moment. To every thesis there is an antithesis, and to this there is a synthesis. Truth is thus a never-dying process. We then know the meaning of the statement attributed to Leibnitz: "I would walk twenty miles to listen to my worst enemy if I could learn something."

Rollo May

A Measure of Success

Children have a way of cutting through to the heart of an issue and showing an unbiased and objective view of things.

A good friend of mine, Bill Mazanec, an executive of a savings and loan association, told me a story about an exercise his son was asked to do for school.

The boy was told to write a sentence about his family. So after dinner one evening he went to his room and began working on the project. In a few minutes he came to his mother with a carefully printed sentence that read: "We are rich."

Well, his mother obviously did not want a sentence like that going around school so she tried to explain to the boy that though his father worked for a financial institution it did not automatically mean they were rich....

The boy returned to his room to try again. In a few

moments he returned with another sentence which read: "We are poor."

Well, by this time, Bill and his wife realized that some further explanation was required. They explained that they were not poor either. Just because you are not rich does not mean that you are poor. They were some place in between.

Well, the youngster returned to his room for a third try. He came down again with the sentence: "We are happy."...

When this story was related to me I knew at once that I was talking to the head of a successful family. His son had perceived the object of true success — happiness. It is true that we have to insure good health, education, shelter, and a sufficient amount of food, but success is not measured by material things. It is measured by the feeling of contentment, happiness, and well-being that comes from the way you live.

Nelson Boswell

I have never, not this day nor since, nor at any time in my life, been willing to believe that I have done *all* I could. But I know that it is nothing to succeed if one has not taken great trouble; and it is nothing to fail if one has done the best one could.

Nadia Boulanger

The world is all new—
all the time.

The Need to Create

In his book Heroes, *Joe McGinniss asks writer Arthur Miller why he still labors to create. Mr. Miller explains this and tells why creating is a never-ending process.*

Supposedly, you do it [create] for your peers. But I have no peers any more. They're all gone. I do it because I have to do it. Because I can't bear living without it. The earlier impulses of proving yourself and of competing can only carry you so far. Then you realize that practically all of it is transient. Written, produced, acted, and gone. If you keep going after that, I guess it's because you need to try to make something beautiful. To give form to the chaos of feeling that is your life.

The problem is, you can never stop and say: "There, I've got it." The world is all new all the time. I go out there, and every day I'm starting all over again. I'm always an amateur. I start something, and then I realize I simply don't know how to do it. Every day I give up. But then I always come back to it again.

Controlled hysteria is what's required. To exist constantly in a state of controlled hysteria. It's agony. But everyone has agony. The difference is that I try to take my agony home and teach it to sing.

Always a New Purpose

From the time that our remote ancestor picked up his first stick or bone fragment to use as a tool, man began to use his potential power of inventiveness that has developed over thousands of years into the production today of tools of unbelievable refinement. Along with this capacity has gone the human need to adorn and beautify everything that we make. Even man's earliest crude tools and utensils bear evidence of this desire to decorate and adorn. Again, when calamity has over-taken him and chaos sought to overwhelm him, he has always struggled to achieve order and organization and new purpose. There is something in man, in us all, that will not consent to destruction and death.

Reuel L. Howe

The river flows a winding course to the sea. We must be equally flexible if we hope to reach our goals.

NELSON BOSWELL

Fighting Back

In 1968, Rocky Bleier was drafted by the Pittsburgh Steelers. Soon afterwards he was also drafted by the army and sent to Vietnam. There he was wounded severely. No one thought he would ever play football again — that is, no one except Rocky himself. His comeback is a story of courage and of the need to keep trying no matter how difficult the odds. The 1975 Steelers' Super Bowl victory was Rocky Bleier's victory, too.

It was August 20, 1969. I was an infantryman in the U.S. Army, thirteen thousand miles from home, stationed in Southeast Asia. Crossing a rice paddy, my platoon ran into a North Vietnamese ambush. Small-arms fire pierced my left thigh. A couple hours later, after the enemy chased us into the woods, I saw a live grenade come rolling toward me. I started to jump...it exploded. I had shrapnel blown up both legs, and several shattered bones in my right foot....

In a hospital several days later, I told the doctor I was a professional football player. I told him to give it to me straight. What did he think were my chances of playing again?

He didn't even want to talk about football. He wanted to talk about walking normally again.

For seven months, there were crutches, and canes, and operations, and leg casts, and physical therapy. When the medical people had done all they could, I put on sweat clothes and went out to see if I was still an athlete. I ran only a quarter of a mile before collapsing onto the grass. I lay there panting and crying, thinking the doctor might have been right. But I would not concede.

35

I stood up, wiped away the tears with my sleeve, and ran some more. Then I went to the gym to lift weights. And I did not stop running and lifting, running and lifting, running and lifting...until...well, I still haven't stopped.

For two years, while I was something less than a football player, I stuck around through an incredible combination of circumstances and the benevolence of Arthur J. Rooney, Sr., the Steelers' owner. By 1972, I was capable again. Slowly, agonizingly, I progressed. And now, today, I'm ready to strap on my hat for the biggest football game in the world.

This is the game that will make my odyssey complete. Seventy-five million people will be watching — more people than have seen any sporting event, moon shot, assassination, impeachment, or coronation....

And yet, I already have more than the Super Bowl can give me. I have an experience. A singular, highly personal experience.

I have the memory of those first, horrifying weeks, when nothing seemed to work....

I have the memory of an alarm clock stirring me up at 5:30 A.M. It was dark and cold outside. My body was still sore from yesterday, and the day before, and the day before that. Something inside me said, "Later. You can do that workout later. This afternoon or tonight. Go back to bed."

I have the memory of resisting those temptations on a thousand painful mornings; of seeing a thousand different sunrises while I ran myself to the brink of exhaustion; of finishing a workout, my skin tingly with perspiration, my legs wobbling unsteadily, my head feeling light and faint, my lungs gulping and gasping....

Ultimately, I did it all for myself. I did it so I couldn't

ask myself, ten years later, "What if I'd rehabilitated? What if I'd gotten into super condition? Could I have made the team?"

Through the whole ordeal, I was at peace with myself. My fulfillment — strangely, almost masochistically — was in the workouts, in the sweat, in the ache, in conquering the 5:30 A.M. temptations. I was content merely to try, even if I never played another minute of professional football.

We act as though comfort and luxury were the chief requirements of life, when all we need to make us really happy is something to be enthusiastic about.

CHARLES KINGSLEY

Stuff You Can't Buy

Elizabeth Ashley tells why she loves her work — why she became, and continues to be, an actress.

When I was a very young actress somebody told me that if I really got lucky, maybe once in my life I would do something that was the reason that you became an actress in the first place, on the high side. Mainly, it's on the low side. [*Cat on a Hot Tin Roof* at Stratford in 1974] was the highest gig I ever did in my life. It gave me something of myself I hadn't been able to claim before, and I began to really love myself and my life and my work. And I came to know that it's not all nickel, dime, pigs and swine, con men, shill games and flat store stands. It mostly is. They own the world. But there's still stuff they can't buy. It's dreams. It's magic. It's love. It's art. It's honesty. It's compassion. The success pushers have got all the real estate. But there are still edges that they don't own and all I want is to be able to live there. Do you know what I mean?

Believing in Yourself

One of the most important lessons I've learned is: nobody will believe in you unless you believe in yourself first. If a person doubts his own ability, how can he convince others of his worth? I surround myself with positive-thinking people and try to remember that you always have to keep topping yourself.

Liberace

A Step Forward

The famous entertainer Lawrence Welk explains how a positive approach can help us reach our goals.

We teach through a combination of love, encouragement, and example. Love — an honest concern for the other person — has always been an unparalleled way to develop people, of course. But encouragement is of vital importance, too.

So when any of our kids takes a step forward, no matter how small, I make it a point to compliment and encourage him. I learned a long time ago that a well-placed word of praise can motivate far better than criticism. I'd say the key word is "positive." We try always to stay on the positive side.

And I've always believed that simply *believing* in someone can be the best way in the world to encourage him. Everything has to start in the mind first...it has to happen there. If you believe in someone else's talents strongly enough, pretty soon he'll begin to believe, too, and the results can be nothing short of miraculous. (It works on yourself, too. All my life, I've set up a goal, a dream, and then I believe, with absolute confidence, that I'll make it. And so many times I do. In fact, my daughter Donna once said thoughtfully, "You know, Dad, we Welks aren't so talented. Just persistent!" She has a point.)

COURAGE

The acorn becomes an oak by means of automatic growth; no commitment is necessary. The kitten similarly becomes a cat on the basis of instinct. NATURE and BEING are identical in creatures like them. But a man or woman becomes fully human only by his or her choices and his or her commitment to them. People attain worth and dignity by the multitude of decisions they make from day by day. These decisions require courage.

ROLLO MAY

Say Yes to Yourself

From childhood on I wanted to hear that applause, get total acceptance for a minute or two. Sometimes I used to feel better as a character than I did as myself. Acting makes me feel right. Rather than always questioning myself, I see who I am. I can say, "Hey, come on, you're all right! So what if you don't get this movie or that one, or so-and-so doesn't call?" And it works. It took me until a couple of years ago when I was twenty-seven to learn that you can say yes to yourself. You don't need anybody else to approve of your life.

Cindy Williams

We all want to be a success in life. Some achieve heights of fame in their fields, others live quiet lives. Yet who can say that they are not equally successful?

ESTHER YORK BURKHOLDER

Everybody Is a Star

Seventeen-year-old Kevin Hooks is a successful actor, with roles in Sounder, JT *and* Aaron Loves Angela *to his credit. Here he talks about star quality — the kind everyone can have!*

I wear a star on a chain around my neck. My mother gave it to me for my sixteenth birthday, after asking me what I wanted. When most people see it they say, "Oh, you think you're a star!" But that's not why I wear it. I wear it because I think everyone, no matter who, has some quality that makes him or her unique, just as every star is unique. In essence everybody is a star. Most people don't recognize that.

I knew someone once who was hooked up in drugs, a gang leader. To everybody else he was a bad guy, but I used to talk to him and we did things together. We were pretty good friends. He finally went off to jail for a year, and when he came out, he had developed this ability to work with wood. He made some of the most beautiful tabletops I've ever seen. I still have a couple of them. He started getting into other things like writing; he began to rehabilitate himself just from finding out in jail that he could work with wood. Everybody has some kind of quality. When people ask me about the star, that's what I tell them, so they'll realize they have something too.

My journey to tomorrow
is always just beginning....

The Journey to Tomorrow

"Don't you ever get bored in the country in winter?" a city friend asked me.

My feeling is that boredom comes from within and has nothing to do with place or circumstances. There is always something to experience if we have the perception to sense it.

So as a new year begins, I take out my memories and sort them, the rough-cut jewels of my life. I relive them all and then put them away in my special box, laying the dark ones on the bottom and covering them over with the shining ones.

For now I have new experiences coming, new sorrows, perhaps, but new joys also. I have fresh opportunities to help someone who needs it, more love and understanding to give, and a renewed faith in God.

My journey to tomorrow is always just beginning.

Gladys Taber

Set in Optima, a modified sans serif typeface designed by Hermann Zapf.
Printed on Hallmark Eggshell Book paper.
Book design and calligraphy by Rick Cusick.